The Three Little Pigs

RETOLD BY MARCIA LEONARD

PICTURES BY DOUG CUSHMAN

Silver Press

For Aunt Jinnie and her family.
—M.L.

For Barbara B.
—D.C.

Library of Congress Cataloging-in-Publication Data

Leonard, Marcia.
      The three little pigs / retold by Marcia Leonard;
pictures by Doug Cushman.
            p. cm. — (What's missing?)
            Summary: Relates the adventures of three little pigs who
leave home to seek their fortunes and how they deal with
the big bad wolf. At various points in the text the reader is
asked to state what is missing from the picture.
            [1. Folklore. 2. Pigs—Folklore. 3. Picture puzzles.]
I. Cushman, Doug., ill.   II. Three little pigs.   III. Title.
IV. Series: Leonard, Marcia. What's missing?
PZ8.1.L4238Th   1990
388.24′529734—dc20
[E]   89-19717
ISBN 0-671-69349-2   ISBN 0-671-69345-X (lib. bdg.)   CIP
                                                                                AC

Produced by Small Packages, Inc.
Text copyright © 1990 Small Packages, Inc.

Illustrations copyright © 1990 Small Packages, Inc.
and Doug Cushman.

Published by Silver Press, a division of
Silver Burdett Press, Inc.
Simon & Schuster, Inc.
Prentice Hall Bldg., Englewood Cliffs, NJ 07632.

Printed in the United States of America.

10   9   8   7   6   5   4   3   2   1

Once upon a time there were three little pigs. One liked to dance. One liked to play the flute. And one liked to paint. And when they were old enough, they left home to seek their fortunes.

As the first little pig went dancing down the road, he met a sheep with a load of straw. "I'll sell you this straw for a dance," said the sheep. "My pleasure," said the little pig. And he danced with the sheep until her feet grew tired.

Can you see what's missing from this picture?

Is it a load of straw?

Is it a stack of tin cans?

Is it a pile of potatoes?

Or is it a tower of hats?

The little pig built himself a house out of the straw and moved right in. Along came a wolf who knocked on the door. "Little pig, little pig, let me come in!" said the wolf.

"Not by the hair on my chinny, chin, chin!" answered the pig.

"Then I'll huff and I'll puff and I'll blow your house in," said the wolf. He huffed and he puffed and he blew the house in. But the little pig got away.

As the second pig went down the road, he played his flute.
He met a goat with a bundle of sticks. "I'll give you
these sticks for a tune," said the goat.
"My pleasure," said the pig. And he played every song that he knew.

What's missing from this picture?

Is it a crunchy orange carrot?

Is it a green garter snake?

Is it a silvery flute?

Or is it a pink umbrella?

The little pig put away his flute and built himself a house out of
the sticks. Along came the wolf who knocked on the door.
"Little pig, little pig, let me come in!" said the wolf.
"Not by the hair on my chinny, chin, chin!" answered the pig.

"Then I'll huff and I'll puff and I'll blow your house in," said
the wolf. He huffed and he puffed and he blew the house in.
But the little pig got away.

As the third little pig went down the road, he came upon a scene so beautiful, he just had to paint it. Along came a donkey with a cartful of bricks. "I'll trade you these bricks for a portrait," said the donkey. "My pleasure," said the pig. And he painted a fine portrait while the donkey posed for him.

What's missing here?

Is it a mild-mannered mouse?

Is it a tired old toad?

$$E = MC^2$$
$$X = YZ$$

Is it an educated elephant?

Or is it a well-dressed donkey?

The little pig finished the donkey's portrait. Then he built himself a house out of the bricks. Along came the wolf who knocked on the door. "Little pig, little pig, let me come in!" said the wolf. "Not by the hair on my chinny, chin, chin!" answered the pig.

"Then I'll huff and I'll puff and I'll blow your house in," said the wolf. He huffed and he puffed, he puffed and he huffed. But he could not blow the brick house in.

When the wolf got his breath back, he climbed onto the roof.
"If you won't let me in the door, I will slide down the chimney," he said.
"Slide away!" called the pig, for he had a big kettle of soup
heating on the hearth.

What's missing now?

Is it a soft easy chair?

Is it a hard wooden toy chest?

Is it a cold bowl of ice cream?

Or is it a hot kettle of soup?

As the wolf slid down the chimney, his tail dipped into the boiling soup.
"Yeow!" he cried. And he ran away as fast as he could,
never to bother the pigs again.

By and by the first and second little pigs came to live with
their brother. They made their fortunes dancing and playing the
flute and painting pictures.

And they all lived happily ever after in the sturdy brick house.